Strategic Studies Institute
and
U.S. Army War College Press

GETTING TO THE LEFT OF SHARP: LESSONS LEARNED FROM WEST POINT'S EFFORTS TO COMBAT SEXUAL HARASSMENT AND ASSAULT

Lieutenant General Robert L. Caslen, Jr.
Colonel Cindy R. Jebb
Lieutenant Colonel Daniel Gade
Cadet Hope C. Landsem

January 2015

*****

Comments pertaining to this report are invited and should be forwarded to: Director, Strategic Studies Institute and U.S. Army War College Press, U.S. Army War College, 47 Ashburn Drive, Carlisle, PA 17013-5010.

*****

All Strategic Studies Institute (SSI) and U.S. Army War College (USAWC) Press publications may be downloaded free of charge from the SSI website. Hard copies of this report may also be obtained free of charge while supplies last by placing an order on the SSI website. SSI publications may be quoted or reprinted in part or in full with permission and appropriate credit given to the U.S. Army Strategic Studies Institute and U.S. Army War College Press, U.S. Army War College, Carlisle, PA. Contact SSI by visiting our website at the following address: *www.StrategicStudiesInstitute.army.mil.*

*****

The Strategic Studies Institute and U.S. Army War College Press publishes a monthly email newsletter to update the national security community on the research of our analysts, recent and forthcoming publications, and upcoming conferences sponsored by the Institute. Each newsletter also provides a strategic commentary by one of our research analysts. If you are interested in receiving this newsletter, please subscribe on the SSI website at *www.StrategicStudiesInstitute.army.mil/newsletter.*

ISBN 1-58487-658-1

FOREWORD

The U.S. Army has been and is struggling with sexual harassment, assault, and rape in its ranks, but the future can be different. In this monograph, three seasoned officers and one cadet propose a series of steps—based on West Point's experiences—to "get to the left" of these incidents by changing the cultural structures that allow them to occur. This will only become more critical as the Army works on the policies that will fully integrate women into the combat arms, introducing women to sub-cultures that have, for years, equated martial virtues with masculine ones.

Based on their experiences at West Point, they propose five "principles" and corresponding "tips" that will allow commanders and leaders at all levels to think about these issues in a new way. While these principles were forged at West Point, they are applicable to leaders at all levels; inside the Army and out. Among other recommendations they argue that leaders should "seek and break chains of circumstance" and that "education is preferable to litigation." Most controversially, they argue that widespread use of some forms of pornography in Army units can degrade culture and create the conditions for some instances of objectification and violence; therefore, commanders should be sensitive to striking the right balance between unit cultures and civil liberties.

This monograph, and its focus on changing unit cultures to prevent sexual assaults and harassment before they happen, is a breath of fresh air on a topic that has become stale and overly-focused on hour-long slide shows that tell Soldiers how to report incidents.

The authors welcome your feedback on their product, and look forward to continuing to engage on this topic.

DOUGLAS C. LOVELACE, JR.
Director
Strategic Studies Institute and
U.S. Army War College Press

ABOUT THE AUTHORS

ROBERT L. CASLEN, JR., is a lieutenant general in the U.S. Army and currently serves as the 59th Superintendent of the U.S. Military Academy at West Point. He previously served as the Chief of the Office of Security Cooperation-Iraq and as the commander of the Combined Arms Center at Fort Leavenworth, KS. His awards and decorations include the Defense Distinguished Service Medal, Distinguished Service Medal with 1 Oak Leaf Cluster, and others. Lieutenant General Caslen holds master's degrees from Long Island University and Kansas State University and is a 1975 graduate of West Point.

CINDY R. JEBB is a colonel in the U.S. Army and currently serves as Professor and Head of the Department of Social Sciences at West Point. She has authored or co-authored three books; conducted human security research in Africa; and completed study projects in Iraq, Djibouti, and Afghanistan. Her awards and decorations include a Legion of Merit and a Meritorious Service Medal. A member of the Council on Foreign Relations, Colonel Jebb is a 1982 graduate of West Point, and holds an M.A. from the Naval War College, and an M.A. and Ph.D. in political science from Duke University.

DANIEL GADE is a lieutenant colonel in the U.S. Army and currently serves in the Simon Center for the Professional Military Ethic at West Point. He previously served in the Department of Social Sciences at West Point, as an Associate Director of Domestic Policy at the White House, and as a tank company commander. His awards and decorations include a

Bronze Star, two Purple Hearts, Presidential Service Badge, and others. Lieutenant Colonel Gade is a 1997 graduate of West Point and holds an M.P.A. and Ph.D. in public administration and policy from the University of Georgia.

HOPE C. LANDSEM is a senior cadet at the U.S. Military Academy and is pursuing a double major in economics and American politics. She will graduate from West Point in May 2015.

SUMMARY

On July 26, 1948, President Harry Truman signed Executive Order 9981, which ended the practice of segregating the military services by race. That same year, the Army allowed women to join the services on an equal basis with men. Both of these steps preceded (and perhaps helped precipitate) the larger societal changes that allowed fully equal treatment of all types of American citizens in military service. And just over 2 years ago, Congress repealed the Don't Ask, Don't Tell policy, allowing for gays and lesbians to take their place openly in the military.

West Point fully integrated women nearly 40 years ago, with the class of 1980. Since that time, our procedures and policies for successful gender integration have grown and evolved. While we have a long way to go, one of the hallmarks of a profession is its continued efforts to improve. To that end, this monograph shares a few of the lessons West Point has learned on the prevention of sexual harassment and assault. We share five "Principles" for leaders and commanders, as well as associated "Tips" for implementation:
Principle 1: Leaders identify and break chains of circumstance; Principle 2: Education is preferable to litigation; Principle 3: What's electronic is public; Principle 4: Don't ignore pornography; and, Principle 5: Unit climate is the commander's responsibility. We argue that senior commanders should hold junior commanders responsible for their unit climates when evidence exists that bad unit climates have led to sexual assault or harassment incidents. To that end, commanders should personally lead some of this training, and not be afraid to treat all unit functions as opportunities to promote positive cultures.

These principles and their associated tips are not panaceas. However, much room exists for improvement in the Army's programs on this topic, and we submit our recommendations for discussion and feedback.

GETTING TO THE LEFT OF SHARP: LESSONS LEARNED FROM WEST POINT'S EFFORTS TO COMBAT SEXUAL HARASSMENT AND ASSAULT

INTRODUCTION

The Army is in a unique period in its 238-year history: The end of America's involvement in two wars, combined with budgetary pressures that require reduction in the Army's end-strength to a 70-year low of perhaps 440,000 active duty soldiers has created an environment of dramatic and rapid transition. Another of the key transitions will be the opening of combat arms positions to women, allowing the Army and its leaders to focus on talent at each unit level rather than considering gender in assignment. With this change, the Army is now an option for talented young men and women to serve in any capacity, and the military will better reflect society.

While the Army is currently considering how and when to open each type of position to women, the discussion to date has largely focused on understanding the physical standards of combat arms jobs. While this consideration is no doubt important, we must not forget to consider how best to ensure unit cultures truly reflect Army values. This focus requires proactive vigilance across all Army units, not just among combat arms units that are newly integrating women. The removal of the combat exclusion law no longer allows some soldiers and leaders to say that successful gender integration is someone else's problem. The challenge for all leaders, no matter the type of unit, is how best to ensure every member of their organization feels value added and a contributing member to the team, and feels safe and secure both physically and emotionally. Leaders in every unit and organization must establish the right learning environment and culture to integrate fully and to capitalize on the diverse talents within our ranks to maximize unit effectiveness. Successful integration of women into combat arms will require the vigilant focus of leaders and leader development institutions.

One area that will continue to be of utmost importance is the prevention of sexual harassment and assault. To get this right, the Army must first acknowledge problems, which it has to a degree. For instance, the military acknowledges a disturbing trend of sexual assault in the ranks—some reports claim that there were as many as 26,000 cases of "unwanted sexual contact" in the ranks in 2013, of which about 3,000 were reported.[1] Congress and the American people are "fed up" with the ongoing issues, and the military must continue to take its obligations seriously. This crisis has caused the Army to focus heavily on sexual harassment, assault, and rape prevention. This is as it should be: Sexual assault and rape are serious crimes that occur in our ranks far too often, victims have been treated with disrespect and disbelief on far too many occasions, many crimes remain unreported, and many perpetrators go unpunished. However, waiting until crimes have already occurred leaves the lives of victims in shambles, forces many others to live in an environment of fear and caution, and badly damages the lives of the accused, whether guilty of the crime or not. Each case of sexual harassment decreases the effectiveness of the Army in fighting and winning our nation's wars, and each case of unwanted sexual contact changes a victim's life forever. Clearly, serious and sustained attention to the matter is an imperative.

WE CAN AND MUST DO BETTER: GETTING TO THE LEFT OF SEXUAL HARASSMENT/ASSAULT RESPONSE AND PREVENTION

We advocate a holistic approach illustrated by the Army's bitter experience with improvised explosive devices (IEDs). After years of failure in preventing IEDs, the Army turned to a new technique, colloquially known as "getting to the left of the boom." Getting to the left of the boom means taking away the conditions that result in the willingness of the populace to emplace IEDs in the first place. Similarly, we as an Army must "get to the left of Sexual Harassment/ Assault Response and Prevention (SHARP)" and address the culture, language, and behaviors that are the core of the sexual harassment and assault problem rather than just addressing the aftereffects in the criminal justice system.

After describing the perceived and real opportunities and problems, we offer a general framework and principles, using West Point as our case study. For over 200 years, West Point has provided the Army with leaders of character and served as a kind of leadership laboratory—young leaders are encouraged to grow and allowed to fail as a part of their growth process. Since 1976, with the entrance of the class of 1980, women have been fully integrated into the Corps of Cadets. Primarily for this reason, West Point can serve as a key source of lessons learned for the rest of the Army on issues of culture and gender integration that arise when young men and women are put into a military environment together. Second, West Point offers a unique perspective with its identity as both a military and academic institution. Third, it is most closely connected to the Army in terms of its faculty, staff, and resourcing, and the superintendent, who is dual-hatted as the president of the College, works directly for the Army's Chief of Staff. Finally, the strategic future of the Army is greatly affected by the West Point Admissions Office, so it is a great case that, in reality, shapes the Army's future not only through the cadets but also through its rotating military faculty who return to the operational Army after their 2 to 3-year tour.

While the examples used in this monograph are drawn primarily from current efforts at West Point, the lessons learned and the theoretical framework for addressing unit culture can be applied Army-wide and across the Department of Defense (DoD).

CASE STUDY: WEST POINT

West Point's struggle to deal with sexual harassment and assault in its ranks is not new: women have been members of the Corps of Cadets since 1976.[2] Unfortunately, no data are available on the rates of sexual harassment and assault at the time. However, it is clear that what was missing in the 1970s was open, honest communication regarding gender relations. The institution struggled to set the conditions such that honest, candid communication could occur. Today, there is a danger that add-on reactive programs to address human relations can backfire. We certainly do not want to go "back to the future," especially now as we address how to implement the decision to open all combat arms to women. Leader development primarily occurs through education and experience, and West Point has the additional responsibility as an institution of higher learning to ensure a healthy learning environment where the free exchange of ideas is thoughtfully encouraged so that people learn and develop. It is this added responsibility and identity as an institution of higher learning that provides West Point with an opportunity to lead change in our Army, and in this case, to lead the effort to successfully integrate women in the combat arms.

If the Army is going to change its culture, we will have to change behavior. And if we are going to change behavior, we will do this through open, honest dialog that allows introspection and reflection. One of the key ways we learn is through communication. Now, as the Army continues to take steps towards setting the conditions that encourage people to treat others with dignity and respect, how do we ensure that we do not inadvertently discourage open, honest discussion—the kind of discussion that very much needs to take place? At West Point, we noticed a potential danger that this dialogue may not be happening because people, men and women, are afraid of being "SHARPed." Why? Because people, in this case, many men, are afraid to talk, thinking that if they inadvertently say something "wrong," they will be severely punished. Moreover, when there is no middle ground for discussion, women do not want to say anything, either, due to fear of reprisals as a result of speaking up about gender issues, sexual harassment, or assault. In other words, people are confusing sexual assault and other crimes that must be reported with sexual harassment and gender issues that in many cases can be addressed at the lowest levels. This is where introspection and learning occur—when people have a real conversation that is essential for developing empathy and growth.

What has complicated matters in recent years is the emergence of social media in the midst of a sexually-charged pop culture. Several decades ago, people could hold a conversation without it being shared with who knows how many people. It is hard to learn with thousands of social media on-lookers who may not even know the context of a conversation. People need to learn from their mistakes—it is not the mistake per se; it is what results from it that counts. We bring in members of the Corps from all walks of life, from all over the country, and from all over the world. Not everyone will come in with the same set of values. This is why the U.S. Military Academy is a leader development institution designed to inculcate values. To do so, we have to set conditions that encourage frank, open discussion. How can Army leaders set these conditions?

WEST POINT'S CADETS AGAINST SEXUAL HARASSMENT AND ASSAULT

Our West Point cadets launched a grass roots initiative in 2011 to tailor the SHARP program to fit the demands and culture of the U.S. Military Academy, called Cadets against Sexual Harassment and Assault (CASH/A). Spearheaded by cadets, the CASH/A initiative has cadets as the primary trainers for other cadets and provides resources to the chain of command in educating others on issues relating to sexual assault and harassment. However, what makes CASH/A successful compared to other programs is that it creates the middle ground by using peer-led discussion in small groups that enables open and honest dialog, which leads to the introspection and reflection resulting in behavior change. Today, the CASH/A program is a formalized component of the West Point Leader Development System, with a representative in each cadet company as well as CASH/A positions among the upper levels of cadet leadership.

The reason behavior change is so important is because our cadets and soldiers come into the Army with a set of values that is either congruent, partially congruent, or not at all like the values of our Army. But our job as leaders is to transform behavior driven initially by the values they come into the Army with, so they are inspired to live according to the values of the organization. That process begins with education, but education only teaches right or wrong. It does not enable values to be internalized. We will change our behavior when we are inspired to live by the ethic that inculcates our Army values. This is a transformational process that we have to first recognize and then lead our soldiers and cadets through. Creating the middle ground where open and honest dialog with introspection occurs is critical to this transformation.

This program is an important step in the right direction, and it is showing encouraging signs of progress. For example, the percentage of women who said that they had experienced sexual harassment dropped from 60 percent in 2006 to 49 percent in 2012.[3] Other positive signs include the fact that the CASH/A program is now a formalized part of the curriculum, and that cadets almost universally report knowing the formal definitions of sexual harassment and assault, as well as understanding the "right way" of dealing with issues related to those serious offenses. Finally, the emphasis on this issue runs from the top of the chain of command of the Army and permeates the organization; the superintendent's (West Point's commanding general, a three-star position) stated #1 priority is to eliminate sexual harassment and assault.

Three years after the CASH/A program began in the Corps of Cadets, we see areas of excellence and areas for continued emphasis and improvement. We recently held the National Conference on Ethics in America and had small group discussion on issues of culture and sexual assault and harassment. We are developing other forums that will create the right learning environment that fosters a positive and inclusive climate and culture. While the CASH/A program has begun to open the necessary dialogue, we realize that we must remain proactive and vigilant and continually assess the program's success. We realize that assessing a change in culture is difficult; statistics on reporting cases are an important indicator, but they do not, by themselves, measure culture. We are reminded of fundamental principles of leadership; culture change requires continual personal leader engagement and an effective learning environment.

HOW DOES ONE LEARN, AND HOW DOES LEARNING CHANGE BEHAVIOR?

Learning is an iterative process. Kurt Lewin articulated it as being a cycle consisting of four points: formation of abstract concepts and generalizations, testing implications of concepts in new situations, concrete experience, and observations and reflections (see Figure 1).[4]

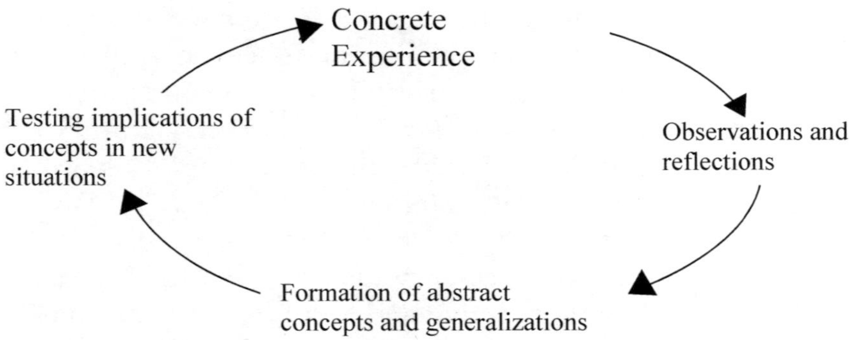

Figure 1. Lewin Model.

David Kolb describes learning as "the major process of human adaptation."[5] Moreover, learning "conceived as a holistic adaptive process . . . provides conceptual bridges across life situations such as school and work, portraying learning as a continuous, lifelong process."[6] He differentiates between performance, learning, and development. Performance is a short-term adaptation; learning is characterized by a longer-term adaptation; and development results in a life-long adaptive posture.[7] While culture change requires learning so that attitudes, ideas, and behavior align with our Army values, how does this learning that Kolb describes result in changed behaviors or a developmental result?

West Point's cadet developmental model provides further guidance. It consists of five components: **readiness**, meaning that cadets must be open and ready to learn; cadets must be provided with **developmental experiences** or "crucibles" that challenge a cadet's perspective; cadets must be afforded both self-**reflection** and structured reflection in order to grow; the process of synthesizing developmental experiences and reflection results in **new capacities and knowledge**; and finally, **time** – development takes time.[8]

Cadets enter the Academy understanding that sexual harassment and assault are wrong and to be avoided, but not all cadets have thought about these concepts in detail. For that reason, they enter the learning cycle in need of help with formulating abstract concepts. The current program does this quite well; by exposing cadets to the reality of sexual assault and harassment and by teaching them the process for dealing with it after it occurs, the "abstract concepts" stage is well-covered. Later in this monograph, we describe how to go about creating positive concrete experiences to cement the abstract concepts stage. Positive concrete experiences within the CASH/A program will develop a core of knowledge that, with cadet leaders and staff and faculty as role models and mentors, will make it possible for West Point ultimately to change its culture to achieve the superintendent's goal to eliminate sexual harassment and assault. From this framework, we offer the following principles that extend beyond the West Point case:

FIVE PRINCIPLES FOR ENSURING AN EFFECTIVE SHARP

Principle #1: Leaders Identify and Break Negative Chains of Circumstance.

A key leadership principle is anticipation of future outcomes: great leaders can "see into the future" and anticipate what action or event is next. An important part of getting to the left of SHARP is recognizing the conditions that lead to an incident and stopping the incident well before it occurs.

The 2013 Service Academy Gender Relations (SAGR) Focus Group Report[9] provides several interesting insights into cadet behavior, among them the fact that cadets recognize that alcohol use contributes to incidents of unwanted sexual contact. One cadet stated that "[seniors] take passes, and they come back after taps [sic] and . . . alcohol most of the time is involved [in incidents of unwanted sexual contact]."[10] Another cadet pointed out that many incidents of unwanted sexual contact involve prohibited relationships[11] between upper class and freshman (plebe) cadets.

Both the alcohol and prohibited relationship examples involve long chains of circumstance before an incident of unwanted sexual contact occurs. Up until the critical event occurs, many people have had an opportunity to intervene. Figure 2 provides a visual description of a hypothesized chain of circumstance: note that at each stage of this chain, there are multiple methods for breaking the chain. Principle #1, then, is simple: all leaders (a term which includes all soldiers, cadets, and Army civilians) must be trained to proactively **observe** chains of circumstance, **recognize** what might happen if the chain is unbroken, and **act** to break the chain.

Figure 2. Visual Description of Hypothesized Chain of Circumstance.

Tip: Train Soldiers on Recognition and Action.

Principle #1 argues that leaders must seek out and break chains of circumstance. With regard to SHARP training, one key element should be detailed, gimlet-eyed deconstructions of actual sexual harassment and assault cases in order to train students to spot the "links" in the chains and identify methods to break them. Just as the Army uses after-action reports to deconstruct combat failures and vehicle accidents, we should use real sexual harassment and assault cases as the basis for discussion and training.

Some of the most successful training uses vignette driven scenarios. Victoria Banyard, Elizabethe Plante, and Mary Moynihan describe their use of vignettes in training: each of the scenarios describes a situation in which bystander involvement may be necessary, and then asks the respondent to identify a) how badly the person needs help and b) what action they might undertake (out of a list of 9 actions). One example is:

> Earlier in the evening, you saw a woman at a party who appears to be drunk and hanging all over some of your friends. A friend tells you she's been taken upstairs to a bedroom, where a bunch of people are having sex with her. Your friend urges you to join them.[12]

While perhaps uncomfortable to discuss in professional environments, such scenarios play out with frightening regularity on college campuses and in barracks rooms around the country, and we should not shy away from addressing them when constructing training. In fact, West Point's use of commercial vendors[13] to conduct some of this training has been effective when combined with cadet leader presence. For this particular example regarding alcohol, West Point is taking proactive steps to address the negative consequences of alcohol over-use by implementing a ride-sharing program, buddy accountability, and formal patrols by unit duty officers, cadet duty officers, and others.

Finally, soldiers should be taught to understand the importance of language in forming cultural norms. Sexist terms should be eliminated, and even gendered terms eliminated whenever possible. For example, all soldiers should be referred to as "soldiers," not as "female soldiers" or "male soldiers." Certainly, using terms to only differentiate females from the "rest" is a subtle form of "othering" such as referring to "female soldiers" and "soldiers." Sexist terms should be thought of and treated the same way that racial slurs are treated. This process has already begun with respect to slurs regarding lesbian and gay soldiers; there is hope for language change around gender as well.

Principle #2: Education Is Preferable to Litigation.

One of the key complaints of cadets exposed to the SHARP program at West Point is its seeming focus on the punishment of criminal acts of sexual assault and sexual harassment. In two classroom discussions with sophomore and freshman cadets, several key insights came to light. First, to broad agreement in the room, one cadet stated that the fear of punishment of a SHARP violation ("getting SHARPed") is so high and pervasive that victims (usually women) are unwilling to say anything to stop harassment, and men sometimes make the deliberate decision not to interact voluntarily with woman cadets so that there can be no possible misunderstanding. The cadet stated, "The punishment for a violation is so great that it causes people to hide what they really think about these issues. As a result, people's values are hidden . . . and the truth of gender relations never comes to light." These cadets groups also agreed, adamantly, with the idea that the "goal of SHARP training is to scare, not inform."[14]

Tip: Train "Escalation of Force" in SHARP.

After 12 years of war, most Army leaders are familiar with "escalation of force" procedures in combat. Principle #2 requires that leaders understand that similar concepts apply in SHARP. Leaders must recognize that coarse and crude behaviors are not, in and of themselves, actions that immediately require punishment. Instead, soldiers must be **empowered** and **trained** to make spot corrections on this type of behavior.

One way to do this training would be in the form of lane training similar to the training practiced for other military skills. We advocate video-based, squad or platoon-level training, perhaps similar to the Engagement Skills Trainer used for small arms training. Each trainee should be exposed to video re-enactments of a variety of behaviors ranging from inappropriate to criminal and be asked to respond. Sufficient responses would be good enough to stop the behavior. For some kinds of infractions, a simple spot correction might be appropriate; others will require reporting to the chain of command; still others may require the filing of a criminal complaint. Teaching and training cadets and soldiers to recognize and react appropriately to these circumstances should and could be a part of any comprehensive program to combat sexual harassment.

Tip: Poor Training Is Worse than No Training.

Poor training is often worse than no training at all because it creates negative feedback loops and habits of mind and behavior that are difficult to undo. In her recent article in *Military Review,* Lieutenant Colonel Heidi Urben argues that small focus groups are superior to "3-hour PowerPoint presentations directed by Headquarters, Department of the Army."[15] Worse still is the fact that soldiers complete the training and then return to their usual environments, which could be places of vulgarity, sexist attitudes and behavior, and other cultural problems. The formal training often stops there, and informal "training" begins, largely unsupervised by commanders and other responsible trainers. The barracks environment and sometimes the home environment may not offer the fertile ground necessary for the positive seeds planted during formal training to grow.

If soldiers have negative concrete experiences, the process of reflection can breed cynicism and other negative attitudes, **leaving them worse than they were before the training**! On the other hand, positive concrete experiences within the SHARP and CASH/A programs will develop a core of knowledge that, over a period of time, can ultimately change the overall culture.

Tip: Training Must Include Positive, Concrete Experiences.

Positive, concrete experiences are the key to effective training, including SHARP training. The training cannot occur solely (or even primarily) in slide shows or other antiseptic presentations. Instead, as Urben argues, smaller groups of cadets and soldiers interacting in discussion-based seminars can uncover important problems and create concrete initiatives.[16] She states that "realistic, scenario-based training that focuses both on how to intervene and how to extract oneself (or others) from a potentially dangerous situation, to having candid discussions about alcohol consumption. . . ."[17] cannot be overlooked in the training cycle.

Another concrete example already in use in the United States is outlined in *Rape Prevention through Bystander Education* by Victoria L. Banyard, Elizabethe G. Plante, and Mary M. Moynihan.[18] The authors argue that the most appropriate method for preventing sexual violence is to empower bystanders to intervene, and they illustrate a concrete training program to do so. Furthermore, their program shows excellent results, decreasing negative attitudes toward victims and increasing willingness to intervene in potentially dangerous situations for months afterward.[19] Commanders and leaders at all levels should feel not only welcome to attempt such innovative training, but encouraged to do so. If they do not reinforce the required slide show-type training with positive, concrete behavioral training, they should not be surprised when negative reinforcement takes place instead.

Principle #3: What Is Electronic Is Public.

The Internet and social media, including Facebook, Twitter, e-mail, text messages, and applications on phones provide invaluable communication and connectivity between people. Unfortunately, there are drawbacks to this connectivity: on-line bullying and anonymous comments on websites and applications can be as damaging as face-to-face assault.

Leaders should be aware of what members of their unit are posting online: it can be an invaluable window into the culture of the unit. Furthermore, as endless scandals illustrate, individuals must be prepared for what they are watching, sending, and saying online to be made public. Malicious hacking, Internet Protocol address tracing, and leaking by close friends or confidants can release formerly private information, images, and behaviors into the public sphere: just as "a weapon is always loaded," what is electronic is public.

Tip: Pay Attention to Private Networks and Online Behavior.

DoD policy already requires commanders to "continue to deny access to sites with prohibited content and to prohibit users from engaging in prohibited activity via social media sites (e.g., pornography)."[20] We advocate a further step: commanders must also minimize misuse of private networks (on smart-phones, for example) while on duty. Active monitoring, including installation of third-party software that blocks inappropriate content, should be considered. Location-based services that allow anonymous content should also be blocked, if possible.[21]

Principle #4: Do not Ignore Pornography.

Another tough, uncomfortable issue that leaders must address if they hope to change the culture of their units is the use of pornography. Although pornography is both ubiquitous[22] and legal, study after study documents its clear negative effects on attitudes and behaviors, including sexual aggression.[23] Among those who view pornography, especially rape and sadomasochistic pornography, men:

> report a greater likelihood of raping, committing sexual assault, higher rape myth acceptance, lower willingness to intervene in a sexual assault situation, and lower efficacy to intervene in a sexual assault situation.[24]

> The large body of research on pornography functions as a teacher of, a permission-giver for, and a trigger of many negative behaviors and attitudes that can severely damage not only the users but many others, including strangers. The damage is seen in men, women, and children, and in both married and single adults. It involves pathological behaviors, illegal behaviors, and some behaviors that are both illegal and pathological. Pornography is an equal opportunity and very lethal toxin.[25]

We acknowledge this is a difficult topic, which is why it deserves a leader's attention.

Tip: Commanders Should Consider Designating Barracks as Workspaces.

Certain barracks, particularly those at West Point or in deployed environments, double as working spaces and living spaces. At West Point, for example, cadets have computers and desks in their rooms and no access to a separate office space. For that reason, commanders should consider designating those spaces as work areas, and consider applying the same standards to pornographic materials in those spaces that they would in other work areas. This is clearly a sensitive area, but ample precedent exists: General Order #1 for deployed forces prohibits purchasing, producing, or displaying any pornographic or sexually explicit material, including on electronic storage devices.[26]

Principle #5: Unit Climate Is the Commander's Responsibility.

While this principle may be a statement of the obvious, it is worth explicitly stating. Unit commanders in the Army have immense responsibility: they are responsible for the health, welfare, training, and combat employment of their unit. Furthermore, they have Uniform Code of Military Justice authority over their soldiers. Colloquially, commanders are said to be responsible for everything that "does or does not happen in their units." Given this broadly-held cultural and legal understanding, commanders must be held responsible for the unit climate, including the climate of gender relations in their unit. Moreover, unit commanders must be personally engaged in SHARP training; it should not be someone else's extra duty.

Tip: Evaluate Commanders on Unit Climate & Hold Them Accountable.

Given that the commander must be held accountable for all aspects of the unit culture, we suggest that the unit commanders must be trained and expected to **personally lead** anti-sexual assault and harassment training whenever possible. There is simply no substitute for personal leadership during high-value training. Company commanders and other leaders must be held accountable for any part of the unit climate or unit activities that facilitate or fail to prevent sexual assault and harassment.[27] Any event in which all or a significant portion of unit members participate, whether on or off-installation, should be treated as a function subject to military cultural expectations. This accountability includes activities in the barracks during off-duty hours, the social events that units plan, and any other area in which "army life" extends.

CONCLUSION

During the next few years, units across the Army will continue to integrate women into new positions. At West Point, we just accepted the highest percentage of women in its history with the entering Class of 2018—21 percent. It is absolutely critical that a number of different issues inherent to this transition are addressed; perhaps chief among them is the culture required to ensure absolute trust among teammates, space for dialogue, and no tolerance for intentional and vicious sexual harassment and certainly none for assault. In short, leaders need to get to the *Left of SHARP.*

We at West Point, and commanders and leaders in the larger Army, must set the conditions within our units where every one of our soldiers or cadets feel value added, are treated with dignity and respect, and are secure both physically and emotionally. Our leaders and commanders must continue to be open and honest about which efforts are successful and which are not as we attempt to eliminate sexual harassment and assault. Our current program, while very good in some respects, will benefit from continued maturation. Our goal is not simply to stamp out instances of sexual harassment and assault, but to make fundamental cultural changes which will result in sexual harassment and assault being foreign to the experience of the average cadet. Using another analogy, we seek to alter the DNA of our unit, changing the culture so that each soldier or cadet is able to act as an antibody to the infection of sexual harassment and assault.

As we continue to improve our programs at West Point, we humbly offer lessons learned to the larger Army about our experiences thus far.

REFERENCES

Banyard, Victoria L., Elizabethe G. Plante, and Mary M. Moynihan. "Rape Prevention Through Bystander Education: Bringing a Broader Community Perspective to Sexual Violence Prevention." Washington, DC: U.S. Department of Justice, 2005. Available from *https://www.ncjrs.gov/pdffiles1/nij/grants/208701.pdf.*

Defense Manpower Data Center. "2013 Service Academy Gender Relations Focus Groups." Fort Belvoir, VA: Defense Technical Information Center. 2013. Available from *www.sapr.mil/public/docs/research/2013_sagr_focus_group_report.pdf.*

Foubert, John D., Matthew W. Brosi, and R. Sean Bannon. "Pornography Viewing among Fraternity Men: Effects on Bystander Intervention, Rape Myth Acceptance and Behavioral Intent to Commit Sexual Assault," *Sexual Addiction & Compulsivity: The Journal of Treatment & Prevention*, Vol. 18, No. 4, pp. 212-231.

General Order Number 1 (GO-1). Headquarters, Multi-National Corps-Iraq. April 4, 2009. Available from *lawprofessors.typepad.com/files/go-1.pdf.* (accessed July 15, 2014).

Kolb, David A. *Experiential Learning: Experience as the Source of Learning Development.* Englewood Cliffs, New Jersey: Prentice-Hall, Inc., 1984.

Layden, Mary Anne. "Pornography and Violence: A New look at the Research." James R. Stone Jr. and Donna M. Hughes, eds., *The Social Costs of Pornography,* Princeton, NJ: The Witherspoon Institute. 2010.

Newton-Small, Jay. "McCaskill Set to Win the Battle on Sexual Assault in the Military." Available from *time.com/18355/mccaskill-set-to-win-the-battle-on-sexual-assault-in-the-military/* (accessed March 18, 2014).

Office of the Deputy Secretary of Defense. "Directive-Type Memorandum (DTM) 09-026- Responsible and Effective Use of Internet-based Capabilities." February 25, 2010.

United States Military Academy Academic Affairs Division. "Building Capacity to lead: The West Point System for Leader Development," 2009. Available from *www.usma.edu/strategic/site-assets/sitepages/home/building%20the%20capacity%20to%20lead.pdf.*

Urben, Heidi. "Extending SHARP Best Practices." *Military Review*. March-April 2014, pp. 29-32.

Vega, Vanessa and Neil M. Malamuth. "Predicting Sexual Aggression: The Role of Pornography in the Context of General and Specific Risk Factors," *Aggressive Behavior* Vol. 33, No. 2, pp. 104-117.

ENDNOTES

1. Jay Newton-Small, "McCaskill Set to Win the Battle on Sexual Assault in the Military," *Time,* March 10, 2014, available from *time.com/18355/mccaskill-set-to-win-the-battle-on-sexual-assault-in-the-military/.*

2. One of the authors of this monograph was a member of the third class to admit women. All of the problems we outline here were problems then as well.

3. These data, which are the most recent available, is drawn from the *2013 Service Academy Gender Relations Report*, available from *www.sapr.mil/public/docs/research/2013_sagr_focus_group_report.pdf.*

4. David A. Kolb, *Experiential Learning: Experience as the Source of Learning Development,* Englewood Cliffs, NJ: Prentice-Hall, 1984, pp. 21-22, available from *academic.regis.edu/ed205/kolb.pdf.* The Lewin model is taken from Figure 2.1, p. 21.

5. *Ibid.*, p. 32.

6. *Ibid.*, p. 33.

7. *Ibid.*, p. 34.

8. "Building Capacity to Lead: The West Point System for Leader Development," West Point, NY: United States Military Academy, 2009, pp. 13-14.

9. *Service Academy Gender Relations Focus Group Report.* Alexandria, VA: Defense Manpower Data Center, 2013.

10. *Ibid.*, p. 10.

11. We deliberately do not use the technical term "fraternization" (*Army Regulation (AR) 600-20*, Para. 4-16) because its etymology in the French word "*fraterniser*" is entirely positive, meaning "to sympathize as brothers." After 1897, it began to mean friendship with enemy troops, and only during World War II did it begin to mean "sex with women from enemy countries." Its ongoing

use in the U.S. Army as a catch-all term for improper senior-subordinate relationships should be reconsidered.

12. Victoria L. Banyard, Elizabethe G. Plante, and Mary M. Moynihan, "Rape Prevention Through Bystander Education: Bringing a Broader Community Perspective to Sexual Violence Prevention," Washington, DC: U.S. Department of Justice, p. 213, available from *https://www.ncjrs.gov/pdffiles1/nij/grants/208701.pdf*.

13. A recent example of this kind of training is the "Sex Signals" training that was conducted at West Point, NY, in 2012.

14. Training session at U.S. Military Academy, West Point, NY.

15. Heidi Urben, "Extending SHARP Best Practices." *Military Review*, March-April 2014, p. 31.

16. *Ibid*.

17. *Ibid*., p. 32.

18. Banyard, Plante, and Moynihan.

19. *Ibid*., 150.

20. Deputy Secretary of Defense, "Directive-Type Memorandum (DTM) 09-026-Responsible and Effective Use of Internet-based Capabilities," Washington, DC: DoD, February 25, 2010.

21. The primary example of this kind of app is "Yik Yak," which is a geo-location based commenting service that enables anonymous, unprofessional, and hurtful behaviors to take place. Yik Yak's operators have responded to requests from high schools to block access to those regions. A similar policy on military installations might be useful.

22. John Foubert, Matthew W. Brosi, and R. Sean Bannon, "Pornography Viewing among Fraternity Men: Effects on Bystander Intervention, Rape Myth Acceptance and Behavioral Intent to Commit Sexual Assault," *Sexual Addiction & Compulsivity: The Journal of Treatment & Prevention*, November 2011, p. 213.

23. Vanessa Vega and Neil M. Malamuth, "Predicting Sexual Aggression: The Role of Pornography in the Context of General and Specific Risk Factors," *Aggressive Behavior*, Vol. 33, No. 2, pp. 104-117.

24. Foubert, Brosi, and Bannon, p. 225.

25. Mary Anne Layden, "Pornography and Violence: A New Look at the Research," James R. Stone, Jr., and Donna M. Hughes, eds., *The Social Costs of Pornography*, Princeton, NJ: The Witherspoon Institute, 2010, p. 61.

26. General Order Number 1 (GO-1). Headquarters, Multi-National Corps-Iraq, April 4, 2009.

27. In a recent case, the leadership of a West Point class faced a dilemma about whether to invite the scantily-clad "Bud Light Girls" to a social function at the club reserved for them on-post. The principle of "commanders are responsible for the unit's functions, on and off duty" would have helped guide their decision-making on this point.

U.S. ARMY WAR COLLEGE

Major General William E. Rapp
Commandant

*****

STRATEGIC STUDIES INSTITUTE
and
U.S. ARMY WAR COLLEGE PRESS

Director
Professor Douglas C. Lovelace, Jr.

Director of Research
Dr. Steven K. Metz

Authors
Lieutenant General Robert L. Caslen, Jr.
Colonel Cindy R. Jebb
Lieutenant Colonel Daniel Gade
Cadet Hope C. Landsem

Editor for Production
Dr. James G. Pierce

Publications Assistant
Ms. Rita A. Rummel

*****

Composition
Mrs. Jennifer E. Nevil

STRATEGIC STUDIES INSTITUTE

The Strategic Studies Institute (SSI) is part of the U.S. Army War College and is the strategic-level study agent for issues related to national security and military strategy with emphasis on geostrategic analysis.

The mission of SSI is to use independent analysis to conduct strategic studies that develop policy recommendations on:

- Strategy, planning, and policy for joint and combined employment of military forces;
- Regional strategic appraisals;
- The nature of land warfare;
- Matters affecting the Army's future;
- The concepts, philosophy, and theory of strategy; and,
- Other issues of importance to the leadership of the Army.

Studies produced by civilian and military analysts concern topics having strategic implications for the Army, the Department of Defense, and the larger national security community.

In addition to its studies, SSI publishes special reports on topics of special or immediate interest. These include edited proceedings of conferences and topically oriented roundtables, expanded trip reports, and quick-reaction responses to senior Army leaders.

The Institute provides a valuable analytical capability within the Army to address strategic and other issues in support of Army participation in national security policy formulation.

The United States Army War College

The United States Army War College educates and develops leaders for service at the strategic level while advancing knowledge in the global application of Landpower.

The purpose of the United States Army War College is to produce graduates who are skilled critical thinkers and complex problem solvers. Concurrently, it is our duty to the U.S. Army to also act as a "think factory" for commanders and civilian leaders at the strategic level worldwide and routinely engage in discourse and debate concerning the role of ground forces in achieving national security objectives.

The Strategic Studies Institute publishes national security and strategic research and analysis to influence policy debate and bridge the gap between military and academia.

The Center for Strategic Leadership and Development contributes to the education of world class senior leaders, develops expert knowledge, and provides solutions to strategic Army issues affecting the national security community.

The Peacekeeping and Stability Operations Institute provides subject matter expertise, technical review, and writing expertise to agencies that develop stability operations concepts and doctrines.

U.S. Army War College
SLDR
Senior Leader Development and Resiliency

The Senior Leader Development and Resiliency program supports the United States Army War College's lines of effort to educate strategic leaders and provide well-being education and support by developing self-awareness through leader feedback and leader resiliency.

The School of Strategic Landpower develops strategic leaders by providing a strong foundation of wisdom grounded in mastery of the profession of arms, and by serving as a crucible for educating future leaders in the analysis, evaluation, and refinement of professional expertise in war, strategy, operations, national security, resource management, and responsible command.

The U.S. Army Heritage and Education Center acquires, conserves, and exhibits historical materials for use to support the U.S. Army, educate an international audience, and honor Soldiers—past and present.